PETER SURPRISES RHODA

The story of Peter's escape from prison
from Acts 12:1–19, for children

Written by Larry Burgdorf
Illustrated by Len Ebert

CONCORDIA PUBLISHING HOUSE · SAINT LOUIS

There was a gathering one day—
Some friends of Peter came to pray.
They came to pray for their dear friend,
Whose life, they feared, was soon to end.

Their ruler was the worst of kings.
King Herod did some wicked things.
He did his very best to please
All Jesus' hate-filled enemies.

For Herod used the Roman's sword
To kill brave James, one of the Lord's.
He then arrested Peter too,
And here is what he schemed to do:

He planned to kill him the next day,
So Peter's friends began to pray.
It looked quite hopeless because he
Was chained so he could not get free.

Four teams of soldiers stood their guard.
The doors were locked and gates were barred.
There was no way he could get out.
It seemed that he would die, no doubt.

While Peter slept that very night,
Quite suddenly there came a light.
An angel came to set him free—
He said, "Get dressed and follow me."

His chains fell off and he arose.
He found his shoes and grabbed his clothes.
They passed the guards and went outside.
An iron gate then opened wide.

Now Peter thought it was a dream.
(In dreams, things are not as they seem.)
But when they'd walked a little way,
The angel left and went away.

Then Peter realized, "It's real!"
Can you imagine how he'd feel?
He knew an angel set him free
And thought of friends he'd want to see.

He went to John Mark's mother's place,
Where he could see friends face-to-face.
(He did not know that this was where
His friends had come to join in prayer.)

He walked up to the entryway,
Knocked on the door and right away,
A girl named Rhoda heard him knock—
And then she got a mighty shock.

She recognized his voice, but then
She ran right back inside again.
She said, "It's Peter at the door!
I'm sure—I've heard his voice before!"

The others in the house declared,
"We all want Peter to be spared!
And we don't want to be unkind,
But, Rhoda, have you lost your mind?!

"That Peter's free? . . . There's just no way,
He's chained and guarded night and day."
But Rhoda said, "I know it's he—
He's right outside, and he *is* free."

Then some said this and some said that;
Oh great jumping Jehoshaphat!
While each friend said just how he feels,
Poor Peter's left to cool his heels!

And then, to their astonishment,
They saw themselves what Rhoda meant.
They finally let him in, and he
Told everyone how he got free.

This hist'ry tells what God can do.
And God cares just as much for you.
His angels still are here today.
They watch you while you play and pray.

Dear Parent,

Prayer is a simple thing, yet it is a profound gift. At His invitation, we can approach the Lord of the universe with any concern and every request. Paul tells us to "pray without ceasing" (1 Thessalonians 5:17). God promises to hear our prayers spoken in Jesus' name, and He promises to answer according to His will for us.

The people of Jerusalem had gathered to hold an all-night prayer vigil on behalf of Peter, who was a key figure in the early days of the Christian Church. Peter was imprisoned at the order of wicked Herod Agrippa, who took delight in persecuting and executing Christians. (Shortly before this, Herod had James, the brother of Jesus, executed.)

Peter's death was likely, and his friends were praying desperately. Yet when those prayers were answered, everyone—even Peter—was surprised. At first, Peter thought he was dreaming. Then, his friends thought it was an angel at the gate. Only Rhoda knew in an instant that their prayers had been answered and Peter had been miraculously released—and she was so excited that she forgot to let him in!

As you read this story with your child, remind him or her that God does, indeed, answer our prayers. He sends His holy angel to be with us, as the traditional prayer says. And through the work of Jesus in our life, He will one day deliver us to the safety of His heavenly home.

The editor